NECK OF THE WORLD

May Swenson
Poetry Award Series

NECK OF THE WORLD

poems
by

F. Daniel Rzicznek

UTAH STATE UNIVERSITY PRESS
Logan, Utah 84322-7800

Utah State University Press
Logan, Utah 84322-7800

978-0-87421-668-4 (cloth)
978-0-87421-669-1 (e-book)
978-0-87421-670-7 (paper)

Manufactured in the United States of America
Cover design by Barbara Yale-Read

Library of Congress Cataloging-in-Publication Data

Rzicznek, F. Daniel (Frank Daniel), 1979-
  Neck of the world : poems / by F. Daniel Rzicznek.
    p. cm. -- (May Swenson poetry award series)
  ISBN 978-0-87421-668-4 (cloth : alk. paper) -- ISBN 978-0-87421-670-7 (pbk. : alk.
paper) -- ISBN 978-0-87421-669-1 (e-book)
  I. Title.
  PS3618.Z53N43 2007
  811'.6--dc22
                                        2007022448

for Amanda, always

CONTENTS

ACKNOWLEDGMENTS

Hearty thanks to the editors of the following publications in which some of these poems first appeared, sometimes in slightly different versions:

Backwards City Review: "Bait"
Blackbird: "During Fever," "Outside the Horse"
Boston Review: "Speakmaple," "Toyhouse," "Genius of Frogs," "Raker"
The Carolina Quarterly: "Stormdweller"
Elixir: "Returning the Ghost"
Fugue: "Primer"
New Hampshire Review: "Nightyard"
North American Review: "Neck of the Woods"
Notre Dame Review: "Grackles"
Paper Street: "First Lady"
Pebble Lake Review: "Crested Daughter"
Phoebe: "Tickets for a Fire"
Red Mountain Review: "North of North"
Rhino: "Mane and Claw"
Salamander: "A Mouthful of Crickets"
Sou'wester: "Blood Realm"
Texas Poetry Journal: "Happy."
Both "Returning the Ghost" and "Grackles" also appeared on the *Verse Daily* website.

Thank you to the many family members and friends who have enriched my life and provided me with the space to write, to the astute teachers and readers who helped to sharpen my vision of this manuscript: Larissa Szporluk, Amy Newman, Lawrence Coates, and Karen Craigo, as well as the following teachers, magicians, and cohorts: Mike Czyzniejewski, Bryan Gattozzi, Mark Jenkins, Wendell Mayo, Matt McBride, Gary McDowell, Sharona Muir, and Christof Scheele. Thanks also to my peers in the Bowling Green State University MFA program who gave of their time and hearts while reading many of these poems.

Warm thanks to Sydney Lea for his generous encouragement and good will. Thanks to Jane Mead and Aliki Barnstone, who may not remember, but were there. Thanks to Michael Spooner and Utah State

University Press, and much thanks to Alice Quinn, for choosing my work. Special thanks to John Freeman, for reading, questioning, and believing. Canine thanks to Sam, who's waiting somewhere.

Above all others, thanks to Amanda McGuire, without whom . . .

FOREWORD

Reading and rereading the poems in *Neck of The World* prompted me to return to and dwell upon the aphorisms grouped under the heading "Adagia" in Wallace Stevens's *Opus Posthumous*. A few of the "Adagia" are as gnomic and unforgettable as the poems in this debut collection:

One reads poetry with one's nerves.
We have to step boldly into man's interior world or not at all.
A poem need not have a meaning, and, like most things in nature, often does not have.
Poetry is a pheasant disappearing in the brush.

Poetry, Stevens noted elsewhere, "makes itself manifest in a kind of speech that comes from secrecy." Daniel Rzicznek's poems cast their spell, it seems to me, because they invite us (like his white crane in the pond in the poem, "Primer") "to the bottom's murk/ silent as snow-melt . . .", to the seedbed of their own making.

"The first successful poems of young poets," Auden said, are "made up of magical lyrical phrases which seem to rise involuntarily to the consciousness." There are countless examples of such mesmerizing phrases here. Daniel Rzicznek writes of the "threadbare light binding the valley" in "A Mouthful of Crickets." And in the same poem,

The dream of the cave is a means,
a must, a smell crawling solid
through the foglike arms of trees.

"Prayer for Fall" evokes "damp swamp light,/ springheeled by the burnt gusts/ of foliage." In "Host," "Winter hangs/ glinting on its hook of light." And from "Hibernacula," "Into the woods the bear becomes/ darkness hedged by darkness." Throughout, the language pulsates, always vigorous, by turns knotty and crystalline. In "Donnybrook," he describes the arrival of a storm in winter,

The opal everywhere eyes
of a lightning-spooled virgin,

branches dangling icy triggers,
the world's envelope open:

extremities numb, a long
and erasing bellow, the onrush,

the tentacles of snow.
Listen: we live each for the other.

"Newness (not novelty) may be the highest value in poetry,"
Stevens wrote. In *Neck of the World,* we have a poet with a striking
new vision--challenging, rewarding, and bold.

Alice Quinn

NECK OF THE WORLD

Sometimes you look for the world, and it's there.

—Tom Andrews

I am whatever beast inhabits me.

—Charles Simic

ONE

SPEAKMAPLE

When there was town here
I sprouted. As the humans
bound a baby, dropped it
to the freezing river, I knew only
that the child levitated, lucent
in some quick vein
of the air's dark sugar.
Now pheasants stitch the edge
of terrain, the pagan wheat
cast beneath itself by sky.
My leaves pause around me,
brittle boats unanchored
to the seething winds.
Loose stretches of cloud ripple
like banners of a bloodrich
city overhead. I place my mark
on the screech owl, the vole,
every heart under my motion,
though the river rules this place—
bones nestled in the alleys
of its trout-flashed bottom—
and I touch the names of arrows
all through this one-eyed sleep.

A MOUTHFUL OF CRICKETS

How do you expect to die
with a song like that, with a riot
of black fiddles among your teeth?

To sleep, to brag of eating them
conjures legs, populations, dusk,
threadbare light binding the valley.

The dream of the cave is a means,
a must, a smell crawling solid
through the foglike arms of trees.

The cavern purges its hollow ice,
a quivering tonsil. Sickles of tar
scan every river of the lips

and it's this thousandth elsewhere,
these well-to-do's, dear. Close up.
Something gleams when you speak.

A BEAR IN HIS MADNESS

There's a burnished violence
ignorant in the leaves,
gilded to the hillside where I sit.
The land has begun holding me
trial for the murder of a sapling
tall as my smallest finger, its leaves
two spots of fire beneath my boot.
The air whirs a mouth foreign
like the speech of far-off bells
in the dark borough of my ear.

There, the lines of brick-lined
streets become sharp
and on a hill beyond the chimneys
(their smoke a thought like this)
he idles, black fur a mass
of gloss, licking himself. Wait.
The land is proclaiming
him king. He rises, bristles.
Treefuls of giant minuscule crows
shake through my eyes like sun.

to coax the shining hair
of dusk down like a rope,

to map a new route
from the wintered forest to

the stadium of rubble,
to fill a stone cup

with the dust that once
was a gladiator's knuckle,

to harbor certainties
about the fish of candlelight

stewing on the ceiling,
to know the inner mouth

as sleek with star noise
among craters and plaque,

to trace the dead man's
handwriting that lopes

with a river's reason,
to witness the river climbing

muddy in its banks,
to know both as breathing.

WITHIN WITHIN

The bear pauses long
enough to shine a dense industry
of triangular teeth.
With each narrowing move
my bones evaporate slightly,
the world slipping into youth,
salmon defleshed into roe,
trees pulling leaves straight from soil
back through the grey armor of bark,
the smokestacks tearing themselves
apart like heartbeats.
See: he staggers underneath,
fattened hind legs upright
as a wiry moth alights, touching off
a depth charge in his skull—
some smoke, tugging waves.
I refuse to exist.

WINNOWING

Between alplike fingertips
a match springs its will
into contour and relief:
whatnots of hill and sage,
the desert night sliding coolly
into the noisy shades
of an open coat sleeve—
the languorous coming-to
of rust and starlight
on emotionless train cars
tugging green and again
green names into darkness.

Still, into the low
carved system of systems
the world dissolves—
minerals scraping skin and leaf
till ghosts of every bone
tilt in some remote heaven.

Still, ordinary sands
shift under wind, thunder
rustles its latent wraiths,
the sky a zero shrinking in.

Hanging the scorched calves
in this plague year, remember
how once we were led here
by our selves, how glow worms
nested in the toughwood,
the knock of death coming
down, every so often, along
the fence, a weathervane
muscling east. Remember
the pines and the blood
in the pines and the dangle
and clack of hooves in the pines
and the blood, and all
of this like green in the bonfire,
the good fire. And remember:
everything acknowledges only
the hanging, the year, and the glint
of earring through branches where
we had marked them, pneumatic
with candor as they were
in the herd's hot center.
How we relish this hanging,
this old way: the hats and chains,
mud dead on the axe's blade,
dolorous winds, and how what
befell them rises heavily up and what
had drowsed in us
stretches, shudders, sets out.

DREAMER IN WINTER

The river ice is hard
enough to splinter bone:
the night sky pinned
to the inside of his skull.
Each try at a dive
takes longer. Soon the music
quits him, winds away
through the snowbound tips
of grass to the mouth
of the road that spat him up
onto the day's tongue.
With caves of wind
around his ears and eyes,
those tools of his escaping,
a fox that had whimpered
beneath an icicled hill
waiting to join him, finds
his brain rotten as a berry,
teeth a fence of bruises,
and the sun breaking on frost:
another restless idea finished,
impossibly happy without him.

DONNYBROOK

A gash of winter road,
blood lacing over frost,

over a bevy of stuck limbs.
When the storm came (spiked

clubs, ax-handled wind)
the wayfarers panicked

in deep puzzles of muscle
strained across fishtailings.

The opal everywhere eyes
of a lightning-spooled virgin,

branches dangling icy triggers,
the world's envelope open:

extremities numb, a long
and erasing bellow, the onrush,

the tentacles of snow.
Listen: we live each for the other.

When my kneecaps leap
with a lion's startle,
will you quell them, soothe
them down like the dead?
And when I have spires
rising from my eyes, will
you turn them inward?
And the sky, when it
folds the diagram of light,
the single, failing number,
will you charter riddles
in four directions? And
when I hear musicians
below, and you, you hear
the love-groans of vermin,
will you seal my jambs
with golden wax? And when
the god comes careening in,
howling for sacrificial meat,
will you have me wrapped
tight in a cloth he does not
know? Oh, will you have
tucked me away, like a stone?

STORMDWELLER

It starts with the call of a lamp
to a book across the room
and the call of the book
to a crippled spider overhead,
the spider not calling at all
anymore, the mute lines
of inquiry growing in half-circles
toward the call of huge winds
wanting to lift the third story
out over the bare mountains,
twist it there like a cloud,
the third story itself calling
to the anonymous thunder
and spinning still inside, the call
of the chair to the haunch,
and the call of haunch to a wren
sunk dead in the rooftop snow,
and the calling of the weathervane
to the kitchen spoons, the calls
of thumbnail to the hammer
and the endless calling of the face
to the skull, the skull calling
and calling, calling unanswered.

TOYHOUSE

A freckled pair of newts
lay dead as trespassers
in the circular kitchen—
ochre fronds open, gills
to a heavens of balsa.

A fly gleams once,
metal green in the attic
with clear stomach hooks,
a tube for glands
and an eye each for us

leveled at our lives,
wooden as we are
and as empty. If only
a little lawn, we think, and
soil hungry under floor—

that we could drop
downward through the rift
to the places longed for:
surgery of slow dirt,
the hues marigolds shed

candled in the earth,
this faith in black thumbs
of lava heaving matter
into pigeons of smoke,
webbed bodies sighted

as pulsing points of coal,
tailbones set like rubies
in dust's sane display.
The core, its nearness—
the killing heat cures us.

GRACKLES

The day is fastened
around the bronze irises

of the grackles as they flash
en masse through the yard.

An airplane's dumb echo
passes over, buzz seeping

through clouds. A small toy
in my gut is coming apart,

the grass pounding fresh
spikes at the sky. One grackle

in the colony loosens
a heavy worm from the earth

leaving a dark inlet
in its place. So these

are the shy, unlit mines
of the body's abiding.

An egg explodes underwater
and you are above water.
Along the map a tiny breeze hurries.

As Abraham began to lose his memory . . .

The snaking of a moa's neck, somewhere
behind *this*. Deeper
inside the breath-snap of a needle.
Water way up in the atmosphere hasn't felt
land in centuries.

I: the baby seal; disabled, returned
ashore by the orcas.
There is again this longing to be
the animal of the wind.
Buddha with apples raised above his head:
victorious.

A painting about foxes and grapes (a long painting,
perhaps). Some buildings
collapse in flame as two heifers
graze in a meadow.

Mangos are floating in the waves.

Juries of quail wait for an answer,
watch your search.

DURING FEVER

Caustic wisp of malaria
    like woodsmoke near the nose,
tumult of decisive blood
    en route from twinkling docks,
a pressing of your figure
    like a handle into the earth.
Landscape remains portable,
    the hills rise into your temples.
Leafy coils roll south
    under black vaults of storm
soaking your rage,
    fading your lids a gradual suede.
The trees jitter above you:
    pin oak, pine, litany of maples.
Roaring sun, imploding roar:
    death like death only.

The tall rushes wait to be parted
and then conceal, when
into the black, muscular length
of marsh the walking becomes
splashing, a tiding that carries
the steely odor of death into the air.
This morning, as we drove,
the first thing our eyes met
was the headless flowering

of a fat deer left in a ditch, until
this final, inked out landscape
where our tiredness is a sound—
a heavy steam escaping the throat
on an east-west road our walking
grinds gently before dawn.
When digested, the land loses
its birdcalls and dens of mud,
turns to a low-pitch rumble:

a water-logged revolving
of trees and necks—the middle
of the mind gone under to a fast
and constant silence. We turn
our numbness to the wind, which
is the sound of a hand in the dark
pulling dark brains from between
antlers, out of the skull, and the eye
that sees them shine, shines.

TWO

GENIUS OF FROGS

In the room drawn from rain
      I've tied maps to the ceiling

to track the flecks of winter
      in each summer's sprung instant,

and the notched, pump-handle tail
      of the dusk-scented phoebe

perched on a gutter the wind pulls
      atom by atom apart each night.

Steel tufts of cumulus sweep
      over my charge and yellows

of automobile headlamps snake
      through mountainways beneath.

I mold a calendar from earth,
      arranging the air's lean mouth

between the sharp flashing of cars,
      the phoebe's broken path of eggs,

and a slew of dewy eyes tug away
      from one another into the prethought

of legs: the coming-to,
      the disappearance at water's door.

HIBERNACULA

A scrap of river glints
its one long diamond of sleep

and the bear turns outward,
believing the water full of mirrors.

Buoyant as stars, his paws
search the slip and heft of rock

and my hands stroll the bed
like minstrels, kneeling now

and then to clench the sheets.
The house-scent carries over the hills,

downstream the moon burns
its coral stuffing in the river glass.

Into the woods the bear becomes
darkness hedged by darkness,

an undoing of pines into
their own dominion. Awake,

my hands rear up, cut and bruised
on slate, skittish as a team of horses

catching the scent of an animal
that approaches, searching out a lair.

OUTSIDE THE HORSE

In saying tomato field one
inherits a green ironwork of stems,
shifting splotches of sun
where light bounds from skin—

with skylight, a cloud
slides back above the landscape—

far removed from saying, say,
landmine: crescent steel, a bed
of red, spent leaves, feather-
width pin upright as a statue—

saying statue one troubles
over a park, pin: medal,

but saying horse a meadow
comes forth, bees quickening
and the thought of nostrils
oscillating eager circles,
hooves still among leaf-spines—

saying horse again, one intuits
a rider, architect of motion,
saying motion the brain is seen,
pulsing along its limits.

PRAYER FOR FALL

Thousands of miles north,
let caribou stir on an open hill.

With five swans lifting
over squat pines, let mute sun
shape the grasses grown coarse
as questions in tundra heat.

Let roads crack through lunar regions
of the down country: hairs
clutching in shower basins.

Let for now a hound to track
his tail into prairies, borders,
and damp swamp light,
springheeled by the burnt gusts
of foliage. The hydrangea,
gut blue beneath my bed's window,
casts petals like bits of map
shredded in the dryer. Let it

barter local roots for what
passes as a life, a name
crumbling free of darkness.
And of course me too. Take me in.

THIEVES

The brain has a drawer
named *home*: the trees shine,
appetite and wonder mingle.
A soldier sits carving an auk
from elephant ivory.
His lips purse downward

in pursuit of the knife's fitness:
the certain peel each slice
rings out toward the handprint
smear on the window, its oil
blooming on the wind. One
door has been nailed shut.

The hand is off somewhere, adrift
from the gripstone of the heart.
A cabinet and dresser
moan in a back room, rocking
the light bulbs into streaks.
The wind dips low in searching.

The soldier knows wealth
lies three corridors behind
the brow, dying slowly as a steer.
The strangers step one after one
to the gates of childhood—
cells shrink back at their touch.

DUST MERCHANT

With each hammering gust
of snow, the scales and thimbles
shrink, and the hanging

foot long folds of my skin shudder
like robes. I may appear
to have wings. I may look

directly past you, remembering
a sheer thigh of mountain
I climbed, in search of an atom

passed through a fish to a man
to a fish—all within a speck
of sand, and that's but one;

the jars here stretch for acres,
the innumerable grains of matter
congregated in shelves, in rows.

This house decides its own name.
I may appear to wear glasses
of steam. I may appear smaller

than before, this weather
arriving on time, my tomb torn
open like the flesh of an orange.

RAKER

The motorcycle meditates
in the neighbor's drive—silver
beyond the silver of fishes—
handles rising sexed
and armlike. I prowl my yard,
flannel replicating in miniature
the dimensions I tend and fence.
In fresh mulch, near the fort
of my shoe, ants weave
late circles. This morning
the glacier fluttered its tongues
again and I foresaw my children
bronzed in frostworn hollows,
my wife shining at the top,
arms silver and crossed,
centering her innards on herself.
But work stretches ahead of me:
many trees here stand dead,
the shrubs need to be pampered,
or showered in chemical spit.
Every fungal face will atrophy
into black suds and uselessness.
There has been a lurching
under the tarp of my skin
and though the glacier has ceased
its mutterings for now, it has slid
toward this country half
of a half of a hair. I cannot
conquer this thankfulness.

SYCAMORE

Old child who
drooled beneath,

slept in shavings
of twilight, sank

with a dark gun
the circles of bats

in a money-pile
the nowhere cows

of morning lull
around. A wake:

windmill glimmer:
closer, now *father*,

a northern train
yowling outbound.

RAINLEGS

The horses all morning
have been moving and moving.
When I bend across
this fence, the grass and my
pores making friends, the fields
stretch their flowered hides.

A guide begins its sprout
in the garden mud: numbers
and photographs maturing
under the soft, green shield.
The horses. I consider this
kindred house an orchard

and my shoulder is the rock
all fathers have carried
a stinging piece of
inside themselves: over water,
and dirt, into the ancient,
lonely clouds. A house

has come nearer. When
I listen, dew buzzes
in her skin. How to stand
in this world, or even
a world resembling this?
The winds go and go and go.

In those pages there's full darkness
and in those long fields, rowing
backwards through the earth, badgers.
And over the movements of plants
about to grow their yearly auras,
a borrowed moon has kept ahead
of a woman and man as they walk,
the man thinking *the stars must be knots
of thread*, the woman: *black sand
behind the stars, black as the back
of his mouth*. Floating glovelike
in the moonlight three geese sharpen
their bodies along fake terraces of wind.
"Lusting for lust," the man says,
"the birds foglike, disappearing."
The woman kneels to a path trampled
with broken stalks, bloodied fur. As if
in a drafty, well-lit room, the stars
bristle and the badgers freeze.
Some of the darkness begins to laugh.

TEN CENTS WORTH OF FOG

Over the facelessness of windshields
and shuttered windows

the thick air twists in
with all the folly of a shark

and the only thing awake
in the newly clouded neighborhood

is the bright branch of my spine.
I am not able to say what

the long ghostly houses want
with this opening and opening: my breath—

but daylight stirs
around the trunks of my smallest hairs

and these lungs flail apart
like twin piles of leaves burning.

The streets remain vague, unmendable
as the fogs settle in,

gritty as homesteaders, questioning
the good of any map

until the churning, brittle erasure
of each garage, every numbered door.

Let me attempt to describe: dusk air
follows the scaremonger's flock
of rumors, his blind horse and black
carriage rattling in the scrambled light
across the only bridge out of town.

Or the morning air: voluptuous gallons
of it between each tanager
perched among frozen fingers of trees—
ruby feathers quietly burning,
the preening of those stuffy coats.

The river changes direction
and the townspeople paint their blue doors
bluer. They junk the lacelike white
of patio furniture, loose their mastiffs
to hunt the potbellied bearcat

to her den near the territory's edge
where there is a chance to mask
the self from all but its mask.
Still, the town floats lost like a hat
in the wilderness that carries it.

We'll need to go before the beginning:
combing the bogs for an oath,
the destruction of the last red
sports car, the scaremonger's clamor,
the barely breathing tanagers.

FISHKILL

The river is a bed of gruel
beneath the leaf-green
bellies turning in mist.

The banks record
shadow and wave,
the noise of light
between ear and frost.

The river is the ear of a fly.
The trees remain blind.
The river passes by a window
of a house in a country
where there is no river.

This waiting for you
has been a stretch
of bark and year, stem
and yellowed bone.

This waiting for you
has been the fireflies'
slow curtain of sparks,
the force with which
the bellies are turned silver,
the eyes stopped.

PRIMER

The white crane
hooks backward through town

to a pond reddish with soot,
wraps broad wings

around its pumping body,
eases to the bottom's murk

silent as snowmelt. Bells
of ancient air collect

in the ears of the man
thought long dead

who emerges now
from his ramshackle house,

who steps lightly
through the rusted gate

to which feathers
have been stapled as a warning.

RADIO

The hum attracts, and just
beyond my ribcage, some old hags

try cooing, flattening
their voices sheer as metal,
chanting the word *magnify*

once, then twice, and on
and on. Then it's *baby*

they sing like this, again, again
and again, hoping that it,
above all others, will gain entry—

the ribs, as they imagine them,
unlocking, my body

in a landslide backwards
and the secret dens laid bare
as late autumn—but

the chest holds. The hags
change the word to *shit*,

a syllable chugging slowly off.
The women become static.
The women become flies.

I breach lightly in my sleep.
This lake shines, is bottomless.

THREE

HELMET IN THE GLADE

I looked beneath:
grass kept the head's impression.

The water I stooped to
was once muscle, organ,

and the body gone missing watched
everywhere: mistook

for shackles and coal the feral
brood of roaches

bursting from the thicket I pushed
blindly through.

My foot gave a knock on that armor
meant for rough

while the alder bed I left
jumped behind me in the wind.

Slow miles of chase and hunger
in the wooded heaven

and I'll never know who turned
the other sick.

We the apple refuse the night,
its muddied trucks,
the world outside the orchard.
We're done with hands,
their shadows heavy
across us. The rain
is what summons. Bullets
drill coves into the air,
their creativity missing us completely.
Somewhere, you are through
with us as well, through with knives
drifting our oceanous bodies
and our hard children
scuttling like beetles down the drain.
The rain. A posture among us:
two flags droop as the soil
below gapes, the midnight crew
burying horses again.
Had we but skeletons
for what once were our wings
before they curled tight to the stem,
we could levitate until sunrise.
Look at us.
When we fall it is straight
and down, the earth swelling a little
to reap our gravity.

WHERE YOUR VICTORY

Figure falling up
in a skyward flail,

the wind turns stone
for hours around you—

head never finding news
of itself, arms

drawing down into legs,
chalk-soft teeth

clacking on air, hair
a subtle tangle of gases

dissipating into anvils
and altars of cloud

until, like the blue
undersong of a magnet,

you wake to a room
in which flowers are dying.

NIGHTYARD

The darkened schoolhouse has
       given me this thing to say:
the dry lips of a man part
       as a candle is lowered
through a glowing block of fat.
       In the top there is a hole
for air to feed in, whipping
       the light. This is the system.
I can feel the cold panting
       inside my navy sleeves.
Outside the butcher's, a mutt
       pisses, the steam ascending
like a ghost after its name
       has been mentioned. But what
is it asking me to tell?
       Our leaders stride sienna halls,
their lilac-scented hands
       flexing. In the grass, a tiny
chant musters itself: *I know*
       you. I know you. This is how
the first, classical speeches
       begin. Then the fat shifts, sings.

FIRST LADY

Whole, the land soaks
pressure like a bandage,
the slow break of time

across the nightstand clock,
the sleet in chains
past the window's swart lid,

pearl wind rotting the yule:
(underwear, cars, underwear.)
Your gown is priceless.

Stung like a rabbit,
you dream your feet stepping
to a country-sized landmine

until in a loose flash
the face-shaped leaves and high
tidal trees release

floating boxes of the dead,
a bastard's returning theme:
text, ghost text.

CATHODE

What passes

for throughness,
for shining invisible

or shy steam
parting from a wound

is now within,
a flick on the bridge

of the tongue,
cavernous scripting

of inner-lung
into a clean remove

unrecognized:
a word for a word

of no significance.

HOST

Winter hangs
glinting on its hook of light
and the bear, bloated,
curls deep in the leafless brush
as the fat, bluebellied snakes
of the sky unfurl
like snakes of fat bluebellied sky
unfurling. Where wild hairs
have kept him like a crib
he whimpers
into sleek shoulders of earth.
Pain has him cornered these nights,
slow force
(chirp of metal on bone)
writing his innards away:
silencing snow the body against
the body of the real against the real
against the snow
its nature of lilt and blame...
Clawing aside the brittle nest,
the sky flowering tongues,
he turns on himself
like a man.

The dim aubades of pears
release, echo around the tree.
While eating, thoughts motion
out ahead in the day's reserve:

the animal must be carried
forth, lured with feathers,
blue song and gun-shine.
For eons we string animals

up (humans, too) and for years
they die speechlessly down
upon us. Someone told me
flesh makes a bed in quiet,

expansive soil, in cascades
of sweat, even some drunkard's
vision of the self as dove.
No one tells me if the dove

can swim, or will be eaten—
eventually. These rank pears.
A watery daughter I hadn't
dared imagine pleads *goodbye*.

HOODED MERGANSER

Little sail-head,
little black wingfish
crowing storm,

I've peeled
livery bargains
from your bones,

worn the shawl
used to imitate
the world.

Ah, fuck and damn
me. Sawbill hunter
for fingerlings,

lake delver
of rainy saints,
rot surrounds

the gold drain
of your eye.
In the harbor

known for waste
and unbeing,
hook your claw-

footed winches,
pull the waters
up into hell.

BAIT

My final mouth lives to eat.

The garden lay ashed, as in rags,
as in crabshell: armor and claws

eightly in unknowable directions.
Each worldly spine lay fitted with blood.

The vitals ache of sun,

two filthy rocks pressured together.
Light folds, passing for marrow;
something cloven, even common

clutching at the downward road
as night passages out the island,
salmon king high in his teeth—

this lord, he will surface as gold.

Where reefs parent a colony
of bombs, the stench of collars
even here; decay ground into seabottom.

The gills lift and rush at the hook,
the crown bones creep nearer,
a shawl spurts up as naiads,

home a wire drenched in skin.

TICKETS FOR A FIRE

He leaves the speckled horse
by the river. Sounds of town
fade like tin as the horse
and he start in opposite
directions. *You are the brow
of wind awake in fervor, in
jungle, in egg.* He stops, casts
a fly to the current. Steelhead,
their berry gills spreading,
waver in the slimed grass.
The sun stays on his hands
and burns. *Selling tickets for
what sermons deem a name
you have defiled, you who
scrawl a map.* And hoofing
slowly, in the way a horse will,
away from the bank toward
a cluster of young birches,
the horse recognizes the sweep
his tail interrupts the flies
with, the rhythm of withers,
the grains in the meadow.

*Snow graduates in skeins
drawn across a land hidden
within the hidden craw,
snow now blurring in the chest
around a foursome of stones
not carved from your parent
but the air's blue gristle.*

*The meathouse's turning
under your decades, a clutch
of great auks rising black
as captains through the ice.*

RETURNING THE GHOST

After the glass of crashing
I bleed into the fields:

water chewing at itself
under icy lids, houses gathering

their cloudy bulks, shouts
of dogs falling over the ridge

with sudden weight,
night turning like a spear

in its own pulsing gut
and the sound that waited:

swish and rasp of ducks
in the bent corn behind me,

flapping themselves red,
nudging down into my lungs,

the air folding us shut
like a blade.

CRESTED DAUGHTER

The daughter of a father
who was the son of a father
whose great, great grandmother
was a blue jay
scraping along a rusty girder
not far from where this page's
mother tree was drawn and laid
like a ship toward the end
of daylight—storm
of boot heels, the bleating of saws,
and all through the earth
the genus slandered the flat homily
of bodies—their one wish:
to abandon the shape,
the formlessness of a shape,
which is why the earth can
be concerned only with this last
blue jay, her harsh squawk,
her color—white under throat, sky
back, the bird gun-sized,
firing cries above the fires,
tucking her feet under, in.

DECOMP

When the gutters fill, you
ask where the rain lives
and are redirected to the worms
who notify the willow-roots
of your inquiry, and I can tell
we're about to get a series
of questions long enough
to knot softly into a noose.
She stole the farmer's only
horse and rode bareback
through the pear orchard;
something about love or a lover,
an interrogation of her body,
how it governs each sense.
It was, at its end, a short,
sad story too immense to enact
here, but details do remain:
she wore ballerina shoes
and the boards creaked like
leather beneath her, and then,
staining the gallows a spot
at a time, the rain through
which she is still falling,
a floor of clouds amassed
around the crags of her feet.

MANE AND CLAW

My dear sisters: how the scent
of half-life spins continual
from our voices like talk,
and the body carnival dumbs

down to calcite: reflective
segments of hair and nail
in us. When the sink drains
the first of me to hear it .

is my stomach—the rust
flying through me like sparrows,
weird marrow nearly dead,
the goat-mask of factory work.

What is stolen from one is
stolen still from another. What
lows in the murk wants, wild and
staring, to pull us enjoyably down.

The fact of night is such:
it breaks. The fact of women
and men is this: the struggle out.
And the struggle out: it breaks.

HUMAN

She limps down the mountain:
pair of hole-ridden feet
clapping leathered mouths on rock.
A button of green wrestles
among exploding coal mounds
and shrivels. She stares at stones
as they flock into liquid,
surveys her isle of blisters
and congregating gas clouds.
The last bird she saw (a blue jay,
a blue jay!) attacked her.
Four thousand years south
where the mudslides of Peru
once hardened over jungle expanse,
the green sleeve, the green ladle,
the green wound, the green teeth
are dusking in the metal dirt
while her lungs like pears rot inward.
Some light lies deviled beneath.
Some worlds won't arc again.

ASTRAL

Between silence and wooden
clap of door, there exist
various routes: you drive off

toward sleep and Orion hesitates
past my roof—its drip
a speech, and speech the train

two blocks east, shriller
than before: a newborn arrow
of air that billows, increases

to familial, moans calm into fields
as space around the town lifts
like a monk ever at dying.

This whole living we've been
within the arms and legs. The level,
fixed light of our pores

whitens, shifts under. The body:
the outside minting allergies—
the inner snowing, and so old.

NOTES

"Outside the Horse" takes its title from a phrase in the last few lines of James Wright's poem "A Dream of Burial" from *The Branch Will Not Break*.

"Dust Merchant" owes a debt to Yusef Komunyakaa's character the Thorn Merchant from various poems in his book *I Apologize for the Eyes in My Head*.

"Ten Cents Worth of Fog" takes its title from a line by Issa, as translated by Robert Hass in *The Essential Haiku*.

"Where Your Victory" takes its title from a phrase found in the hymn "Christ the Lord is Risen Today."

"A Mouthful of Crickets," "Neck of the Woods," and "Host" are hereby dedicated to Larissa Szporluk, who literally compelled me to write them.

"Helmet in the Glade" and "Neck of the World" are dedicated to Amy Newman, whose questions helped them breathe.

The epigraphs are from Charles Simic's "Sleep" in *Dismantling the Silence*, and from Tom Andrews's "When Comfort Arrives" from *Random Symmetries: The Collected Poems of Tom Andrews*.

ABOUT THE AUTHOR

F. Daniel Rzicznek was born in Indiana and grew up in northeastern Ohio. He received his BA from Kent State University and earned an MFA in creative writing from Bowling Green State University. His chapbook of prose poems, *Cloud Tablets*, part of the Wick Poetry Chapbook Series, appeared from Kent State University Press in 2006. His poems have appeared in *The New Republic, Boston Review, AGNI, The Iowa Review, Mississippi Review*, and numerous other literary journals. Currently, he teaches English composition at Bowling Green State University and lives with his wife in Bowling Green, Ohio. *Neck of the World* is his first book-length collection of poems.

THE MAY SWENSON
POETRY AWARD

This annual competition, named for May Swenson, honors her as one of America's most provocative and vital poets. In the words of John Hollander, she was "one of our few unquestionably major poets." During her long career, May was loved and praised by writers from virtually every major school of poetry. She left a legacy of nearly fifty years of writing when she died in 1989.

May Swenson lived most of her adult life in New York City, the center of American poetry writing and publishing in her day. But she is buried in Logan, Utah, her birthplace and hometown.